CONTENTS

                                                        Page
                                    (Lyrics | Music)

OVERVIEW   3   —

THE SONGS

Life Is A Wonderful Thing	4	20	1	16
The Seed Song	5	24	2	17
Spring Chicken	6	27	3	18
Hosanna	7	30	4	19
Easter Jubilation	8	34	5	20
Now Spring Is Here	9	37	6	21
The Chocolate Song	10	40	7	22
Don't Forget (Mother's Day Song)	11	43	8	23
Mary's Song	12	50	9	24
When I Think About The Cross	13	54	10	25
Celebrate	14	56	11	26
Risen!	15	58	12	27
The Gift Of Life	16	62	13	28
Thank You For Loving Me	18	64	14	29
He's Alive!	19	69	15	30

COPYRIGHT INFORMATION   72   —

OVERVIEW

We have compiled the following information and suggestions in order to assist you in making the best use of this new collection of songs. For quick reference and ease of use, we have divided the titles into various categories of theme, presentation and age suitability, and trust that they will help you get maximum mileage from your music.

DRAMA
Life Is A Wonderful Thing
Spring Chicken
The Chocolate Song
Don't Forget (Mother's Day Song)
Celebrate
Risen!

DANCE
Spring Chicken – *costume dance*
Easter Jubilation – *Jewish style*
Now Spring Is Here – *country dance*
The Gift Of Life – *rap routine*
He's Alive! – *ribbon dance*

RE / EASTER PLAY
Hosanna – *Palm Sunday / miracles of Jesus*
Easter Jubilation – *general celebration*
Mary's Song – *reflections on Good Friday*
When I Think About The Cross – *worship*
Celebrate – *Easter Sunday*
Risen! – *Easter Sunday and beyond*
He's Alive! – *Ascension Day, looking ahead*

SCIENCE
The Seed Song
Spring Chicken
Now Spring Is Here
The Gift Of Life

YOUNGER CHILDREN
The Seed Song
Spring Chicken
Celebrate
Hosanna
When I Think About The Cross

LIFE IS A WONDERFUL THING

1 I woke up this morning – got out of my bed,
Looked in the mirror and I got myself dressed.
With a stretch and a yawn and a scratch of my head,
'Life is a wonderful thing' I said,
'Life is a wonderful thing!'

CHORUS *My heart is beating, morning 'til evening,*
I've got the breath of life inside.
My heart is dreaming, I've got the feeling,
It's so lovely when you know you're alive!

2 I went out this morning and what did I see?
Buds and blossoms and the birds in the trees.
With a skip and a whistle a thought came to me,
Life is a wonderful thing indeed,
Life is a wonderful thing!

CHORUS

3 I stayed in this morning with little to do.
Mum said, 'Son, you'd better tidy your room.'
Then a friend came to see me and I was excused,
Life is a wonderful thing, it's true,
Life is a wonderful thing!

CHORUS

4 I woke up this morning and here's what I thought:
What surprises will I find at my door?
With a new day before me and plenty in store,
Life is a wonderful thing, for sure,
Life is a wonderful thing.
Life is a wonderful thing, uh huh,
Life is a wonderful thing!

Words and Music by Mark and Helen Johnson
© 1995 & 2008 Out of the Ark Ltd, Surrey KT12 4RQ
CCLI Song No. 1574802

THE SEED SONG

1   Find a little seed,   *(find a little seed)*
    Plant it in the ground,   *(plant it in the ground)*
    Wait for it to grow,   *(wait for it to grow)*
    Don't disturb it.
    Don't expect to see,   *(don't expect to see)*
    Changes overnight,   *(changes overnight)*
    If you wait a while,   *(if you wait a while)*
    You'll find new life.

CHORUS   *Sunshine will come,*
    Raindrops will fall,
    Your little seed will grow again.
    Soon there will be a day in spring when
    Your seed blossoms and grows.

2   Find a seed of love,   *(Echo)*
    Plant it where you can,
    Wait for it to grow,
    Don't disturb it.
    Don't expect to see
    Changes overnight,
    If you wait a while,
    You'll find new life.

CHORUS

3   INSTRUMENTAL

CHORUS

And that's that!

Words and Music by Mark and Helen Johnson
© 1995 & 2008 Out of the Ark Ltd, Surrey KT12 4RQ
CCLI Song No. 1574819

SPRING CHICKEN

1 One mother hen sat on **4** little eggs,
   Keeping them warm in her little egg nest.
   Then one day she heard a crack
   And a little voice said, as the egg was hatched:

CHORUS *'I'm... a... spring chicken!
I'm yellow and small.
My feathers are fluffy and they're keeping me warm.
My legs are not long so I'll never be tall,
But I'm a real spring chicken and I'm having a ball!
(Chicken, I'm a chicken, I'm a havin' a ball!)'*

2 One mother hen sat on **3** little eggs,
   Keeping them warm in her little egg nest.
   Then one day she fell asleep
   And a little voice said in a whispered tweet:

CHORUS

3 One mother hen sat on **2** little eggs,
   Keeping them warm in her little egg nest.
   Then one day she moved about
   And a little voice said as a chick popped out:

CHORUS

4 One mother hen sat on **1** little egg,
   Keeping it warm in her little egg nest.
   Then one day she gave a sigh
   And a little voice said, 'SURPRISE, SURPRISE!!'

CHORUS x 2

Words and Music by Mark and Helen Johnson
© 1995 & 2008 Out of the Ark Ltd, Surrey KT12 4RQ
CCLI Song No. 1574826

HOSANNA

1   Who spoke words of wisdom and life?
       Only the one they call Jesus.
    Understood what people are like?
       Nobody other than Him.
    Who performed miraculous signs?
       Only the one they call Jesus.
    Healed the sick, gave sight to the blind?
       Nobody other than Him.

CHORUS

Group 1	Group 2
Hosanna! Hosanna!	*Rejoice!*
Praise Him, come praise Him!	*Sing praise!*
Hosanna! Hosanna!	*Rejoice!*

(Both grps) *Lift up your voices and sing!*

2   Who took children into his arms? *(Only the one, etc...)*
    Spoke to storms and made them be calm? *(Nobody other, etc...)*
    Who raised Lazarus up from the dead?
    Made a feast of fishes and bread?

CHORUS

3   Who made friends with people despised?
    Turned the water into good wine?
    Who got people following him?
    Changed their lives, forgave all their sin?

CHORUS x 2

Words and Music by Mark and Helen Johnson
© 1995 & 2008 Out of the Ark Ltd, Surrey KT12 4RQ
CCLI Song No. 1574833

EASTER JUBILATION

1   Easter jubilation fills the streets and towns,
    Celebrations have begun.
    Hear the music and the dancing now,
    Join the laughter and the fun!

CHORUS   *OH! Raise a joyful shout!*
Clap your hands and dance – let your feelings out.
OH! Hear what it's about,
Christ the Lord has come to set us free!

2   Put aside your sorrows, wipe your tears away,
    For a better time will come.
    There's a promise of a brighter day,
    Join the laughter and the fun!

CHORUS

3   La, la, la, la, la, etc…
    (Dance and clap throughout verse)

CHORUS

4   Easter jubilation fills the streets and towns,
    Celebrations have begun.
    Hear the music and the dancing now,
    Join the laughter and the fun!

CHORUS x 2
Christ the Lord has come to set us free!
HEY!

Words and Music by Mark and Helen Johnson
© 1995 & 2008 Out of the Ark Ltd, Surrey KT12 4RQ
CCLI Song No. 1574840

NOW SPRING IS HERE

1 Springtime is laugh and sing time,
It's joining in time, let's give a cheer!
Join hands and have a fun time,
Enjoy the sunshine now spring is here.

CHORUS *Wake up – the sun is shining,*
The earth is smiling, the air is clear.
Blue skies are up above me,
It's really lovely this time of year.

2 Listen – the birds are singing,
A new beginning is in the air.
Shake off that winter feeling
And go freewheelin' now spring is here.

CHORUS

3 Over the pretty meadows
The green and yellows are everywhere.
Flowers of every colour
Can be discovered now spring is here.

CHORUS

4 Springtime is laugh and sing time,
It's joining in time, let's give a cheer!
Join hands and have a fun time,
Enjoy the sunshine now spring is here,
Now spring is here, now spring is here,
Now spring is here!

Words and Music by Mark and Helen Johnson
© 1995 & 2008 Out of the Ark Ltd, Surrey KT12 4RQ
CCLI Song No. 1574857

THE CHOCOLATE SONG

CHORUS *Oh I've got lots of chocolate,*
Give me lovely chocolate,
It's the best thing to eat, for sure.
When I get eggs for Easter
It's my favourite treat,
So I can always make some room for more!

1   I've got some plain and milk ones and some toffee-filled ones,
    I've got boxes all around the place.
    I've got a strong affection for my chocolate collection,
    I'm mad about that chocolate taste!

CHORUS

2   I've eaten milky-white ones and the sweets inside them,
    (I've got chocolate all around my face!)
    They all had pretty wrappers, but that's not what matters,
    I'm mad about that chocolate taste!

CHORUS

3   I've had some sickly sweet ones and some pretty cheap ones,
    But I couldn't see them go to waste.
    I s'pose I should know better, but it's nearly Easter,
    I'm mad about that chocolate taste!

CHORUS x 2

Words and Music by Mark and Helen Johnson
© 1995 & 2008 Out of the Ark Ltd, Surrey KT12 4RQ
CCLI Song No. 1574864

DON'T FORGET
(Mother's Day Song)

1   Don't forget to tell your mum you love her,
    Give her a hug when you get home.
    Don't forget to tell your Mum that she's the best,
    Make her put her feet up – she deserves a rest!
    Don't forget to tell your mum you love her –
        She does all the washing, the cleaning, the shopping,
        And all because she loves us so!

2   Don't forget to tell your mum you love her,
    Give her a hug when you get home (tell her she's marvellous).
    Don't forget to thank her for the things she does,
    Looking after everyone without a fuss!
    Don't forget to tell your mum you love her –
        She takes and collects us and makes us our breakfast,
        She does all the washing, the cleaning, the shopping,
        And all because she loves us so!

3   Don't forget to tell your mum you love her,
    Give her a hug when you get home (tell her she's marvellous).
    Don't forget to give her something really nice,
    It's the thought that matters, not the size or price!
    Don't forget to tell your mum you love her –
        She helps and advises, she gives us surprises,
        She takes and collects us and makes us our breakfast,
        She does all the washing, the cleaning, the shopping,
        And all because she loves us so!

4   Don't forget to tell your mum you love her,
    Give her a hug when you get home (not very likely).
    Don't forget to help your mum with all the chores,
    Clean your bedroom like you've never done before!
    Don't forget to tell your mum you love her –
        She puts up with rugby, she knows when to hug me,
        She helps and advises, she gives us surprises,
        She takes and collects us and makes us our breakfast,
        She does all the washing, the cleaning, the shopping,
        And all because she loves us so!
        And all because she loves us so!

Words and Music by Mark and Helen Johnson
© 1995 & 2008 Out of the Ark Ltd, Surrey KT12 4RQ
CCLI Song No. 1574871

MARY'S SONG

1. I look to the hillside, the skies have turned grey,
   This place is deserted where love was betrayed.
   The life you gave freely was taken from me today.

2. I see it so clearly, the look on your face,
   The sadness and sorrow, the pain you embraced,
   And now it's all over a silence enfolds the day.

CHORUS *Tell me why did it have to be done,*
When my feelings of love are so strong?
Could it be there's a reason
For taking the life of my son?

3. The noises still echo around in my head,
   The shouts and the jeering, the crowds as they fled,
   But now it's all over and I'm on my own again.

4. I gratefully bore you, I watched as you grew,
   I listened and wondered at all that you knew,
   But this is the hardest of all that I've learned from you.

CHORUS x 2

Words and Music by Mark and Helen Johnson
© 1995 & 2008 Out of the Ark Ltd, Surrey KT12 4RQ
CCLI Song No. 1574888

WHEN I THINK ABOUT THE CROSS
(Dedicated to Stanley and Doreen Voke)

1   When I think about the cross,
          When I think of Jesus,
          I'm reminded of His love –
          Love that never leaves me.
          Who am I that He should die,
          Giving life so freely?
          When I think about the cross,
          Help me to believe it.

(Repeat twice more)

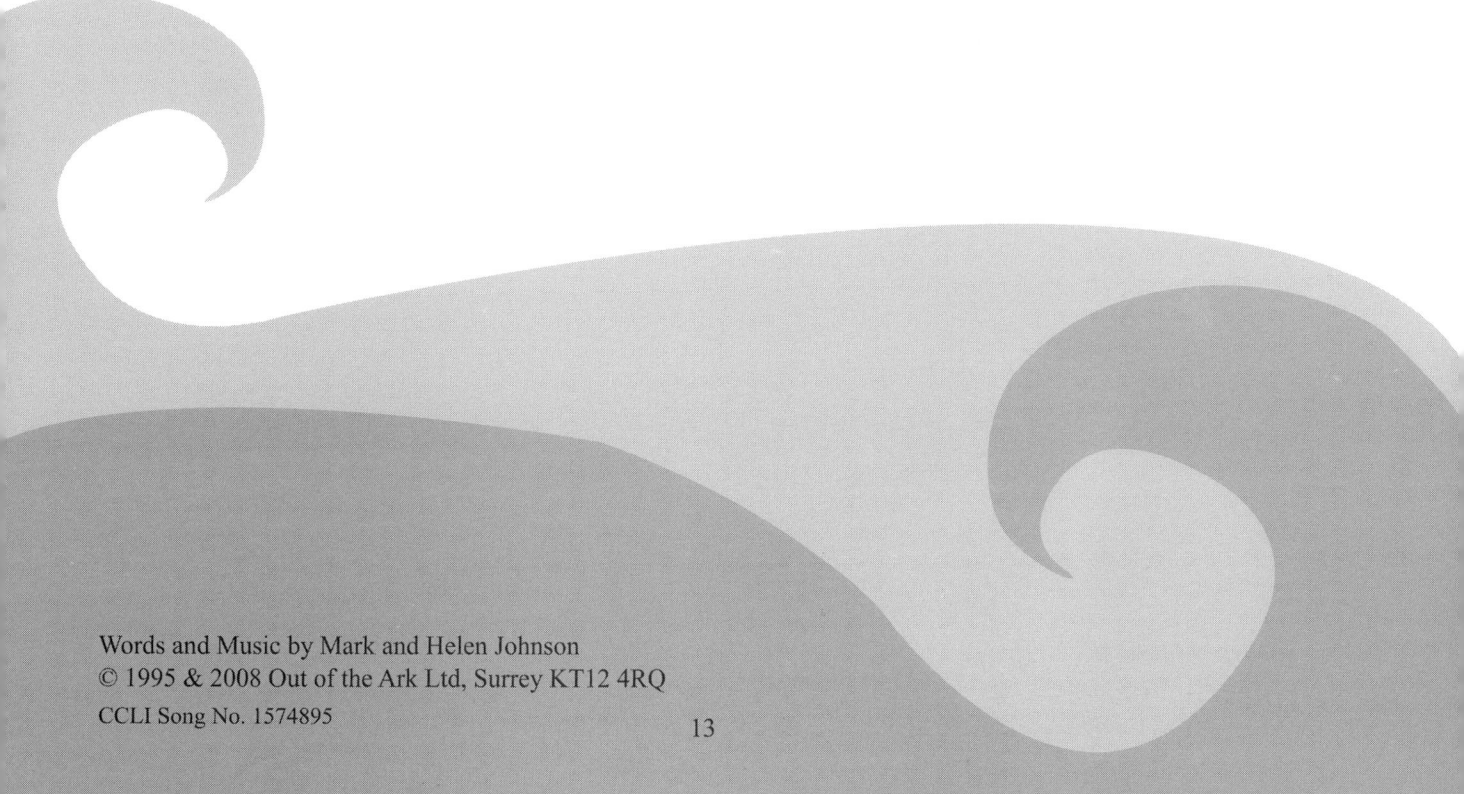

Words and Music by Mark and Helen Johnson
© 1995 & 2008 Out of the Ark Ltd, Surrey KT12 4RQ
CCLI Song No. 1574895

CELEBRATE

1   Sing a song, sing a joyful song,
    Sing a joyful song to celebrate!
    (Repeat)

   CHORUS   *Jesus is alive, you know,*
                He's risen from the dead.
                He was crucified but now He's
                Risen like He said! (Hallelujah!)

2   Clap your hands, clap your hands like this,
    Clap your hands like this to celebrate!
    (Repeat)

   CHORUS

3   Jump up and down, up and down and around,
    Up and down and around to celebrate!
    (Repeat)

   CHORUS

4   Dance to the beat, to the beat of the drum,
    To the beat of the drum to celebrate!
    (Repeat)

   CHORUS

5   Wave your hands, wave your hands in the air,
    Wave your hands in the air to celebrate!
    (Repeat)

   CHORUS

6   Sing a song, sing a joyful song,
    Sing a joyful song to celebrate!
    (Repeat)

Words and Music by Mark and Helen Johnson
© 1995 & 2008 Out of the Ark Ltd, Surrey KT12 4RQ
CCLI Song No. 1574905

RISEN!

CHORUS *Risen! Risen! Jesus is risen!*
The Spirit was given – Jesus is alive!
Risen! Risen! Jesus is risen!
The Spirit was given – Jesus is alive!

1. Early in the morning on the first day of the week,
   Women went to visit at the tomb.
   Angels came and told them, 'The one you've come to see,
   He isn't here, but you will meet Him soon!'

   CHORUS

2. Fearful and excited, amazed by all they'd seen,
   Mary and her friends ran from the tomb.
   Finding the disciples together where they'd meet,
   Bursting with joy they ran into the room!

   CHORUS

3. Two of the believers, with thoughts about the week,
   Walked the road so lonely and confused.
   While they spoke of Jesus and all he'd come to mean,
   He came along beside them with the news:

   CHORUS

4. All of his disciples were terrified to see
   Jesus there before them in the room.
   'Why are you so frightened?' he said 'It's really me!
   All of the things I told you have come true!'

   CHORUS
   Risen! Risen! Jesus is Risen!

Words and Music by Mark and Helen Johnson
© 1995 & 2008 Out of the Ark Ltd, Surrey KT12 4RQ
CCLI Song No. 1574912

THE GIFT OF LIFE

1 Have you ever* stopped to question what goes on inside your body?
I've a notion that some complicated things go on inside you.
If you take a bit of time just to wonder why,
You'll discover there are reasons why we're feeling so alive!
My heart is beating, my lungs are breathing,
My brain is ticking over – it's a real good feeling!
My pulse is rising, I'm energising!
The muscles in my arms and legs are busy exercising!

CHORUS   *The gift of life is upon us all,*
The gift of life is upon us all.

2 Listen to me people what I'm saying is true,
It's a matter of importance that I'm telling to you,
'Cause if living is for loving then you'll only feel alive
When you give yourself to others with a love that's long and wide,
So give it! Give it a go!
Give a little love and then you'll really know:
It's all about caring, it's all about sharing,
'Cause love for one another is for giving and for getting.

CHORUS   *The gift of life is upon us all,*
(All that you've been given is a gift, the gift of life.)
The gift of life is upon us all.

3 I got some good advice from my father and my mother
When they told me that in life there is plenty to discover.
There are places to go – choices to make –
I'll tell you this for nothing, you can learn from your mistakes.
So don't be a bore, go for more.
There's a world around you and it's there to be explored.
Don't stop looking, don't stop learning.
Make the most of living while the earth is still turning.

4 I <u>know</u> it's very easy to get <u>caught</u> up in a hurry
And we'll <u>always</u> have our problems and our <u>fair</u> share of worries.
But <u>stop</u> for a minute – and <u>you</u> will realise,
There are <u>things</u> we take for granted every <u>day</u> of our lives:
<u>Sights</u> to behold, <u>sounds</u> to be heard,
A <u>world</u> that's packed with colour
Full of <u>music</u> and words.
<u>Food</u> and drink, <u>games</u> and toys,
<u>Things</u> to be experienced and <u>plenty</u> to enjoy.

CHORUS *The gift of life is upon us all,*
The gift of life is upon us all,
(It's the gift, the gift of life.)
The gift of life is upon us all,
The gift of life is upon us all.

5 It's <u>amazing</u> when you think of all the <u>people</u> on the earth,
That there's <u>no-one</u> who can ever be <u>exactly</u> like yourself.
So there's <u>no</u> point in comparing –
You'll never really live 'til you <u>come</u> to see that you have
Something <u>quite</u> unique to give.
<u>Heart</u> and mind, <u>soul</u> and strength,
Can <u>all</u> be used together in a <u>life</u> that's well spent.
Make the <u>most</u> of what you've got –
'Cause <u>all</u> that you've been given is a <u>gift</u> from God.

Make the <u>most</u> of what you've got –
'Cause <u>all</u> that you've been given is a <u>gift</u> from God.
(Repeat with chorus to fade)

The title and many of the ideas for this song were provided by the children
in Year 6 at Ashford Park Primary School in Middlesex,
in response to the question: "What does it mean to be alive?"
Thank you!

*All underlined words are to be accented on the first beat of the bar.

Words and Music by Mark and Helen Johnson
© 1995 & 2008 Out of the Ark Ltd, Surrey KT12 4RQ
CCLI Song No. 1574929

THANK YOU FOR LOVING ME

1. Before you made the skies and sea
   Your heart was full of love for me,
   You knew the person I would be,
   Thank you for loving me.

2. You came to earth to live like us,
   With words of life and arms of love,
   You showed the way to heav'n above,
   Thank you for loving us.

CHORUS *Thank you Jesus,*
Thank you my Lord.
Your love came down from heaven,
Come fill up my heart evermore.

3. Because God loved the world so much
   You paid the price for all of us,
   You gave your life upon a cross,
   Thank you for loving us.

CHORUS

4. INSTRUMENTAL

5. So thank you Lord for loving me,
   Today and all eternity,
   And may my song forever be
   'Thank you for loving me.'

CHORUS x 2

Words and Music by Mark and Helen Johnson
© 1995 & 2008 Out of the Ark Ltd, Surrey KT12 4RQ
CCLI Song No. 1574936

HE'S ALIVE!

CHORUS *Come and join in the song,*
Jesus Christ is Lord over all,
And He lives to reign forevermore,
The heavens applaud,
'He's alive! He's alive!'

1. Lift your hearts and your voices,
Fill the earth with rejoicing for
He's ascended to the skies,
In heaven now He reigns.
Lord of glory, Lord of life,
He will return again!

CHORUS

2. Lift your hearts and your voices,
Fill the earth with rejoicing for
Every knee shall bow to Him
And everyone confess:
Jesus Christ is Lord and King,
He's conquered sin and death!

CHORUS

3. Lift your hearts and your voices,
Fill the earth with rejoicing for
Every nation, every tribe
Will glorify His name.
All creation shall bow down
And honour Him with praise!

CHORUS *Come and join in the song,*
Jesus Christ is Lord over all,
And He lives to reign forevermore,
The heavens applaud,
"He's alive! He's alive!
He's alive! He's alive!"

Words and Music by Mark and Helen Johnson
© 1995 & 2008 Out of the Ark Ltd, Surrey KT12 4RQ
CCLI Song No. 1574943

LIFE IS A WONDERFUL THING

*Words and Music by
Mark and Helen Johnson*

With energy, with a swing ♩ = 132

woke up this morn-ing — got out of my bed,
(2.) went out this morn-ing and what did I see?
(3.) stayed in this morn-ing with lit-tle to do,

© 1995 & 2008 Out of the Ark Ltd, Surrey KT12 4RQ
CCLI Song No. 1574802

looked in the mir-ror and I got my-self dressed. With a
Buds and blos-soms and the birds in the trees. With a
Mum said 'Son, you'd bet-ter ti-dy your room'. Then a

stretch and a yawn and a scratch of my head,
skip and a whis-tle a thought came to me,
friend came to see me and I was ex-cused,

'Life is a won-der-ful thing' I said, 'Life is a won-der-ful thing!'
life is a won-der-ful thing in-deed, life is a won-der-ful thing!
life is a won-der-ful thing, it's true, life is a won-der-ful thing!

My heart is beat-ing, morn - ing 'til eve-ning,
I've got the breath of life in - side. My heart is dream-ing, I've
got the feel-ing, it's so love-ly when you know you're a - live!

2. I
3. I

know you're a - live! 4. I woke up this morn-ing and here's what I thought:

What sur-pri-ses will I find at my door? With a new day be-fore me and plen-ty in store, life is a won-der-ful thing, for sure, life is a won-der-ful thing. Life is a won-der-ful thing, uh huh, life is a won-der-ful thing!

THE SEED SONG

Words and Music by
Mark and Helen Johnson

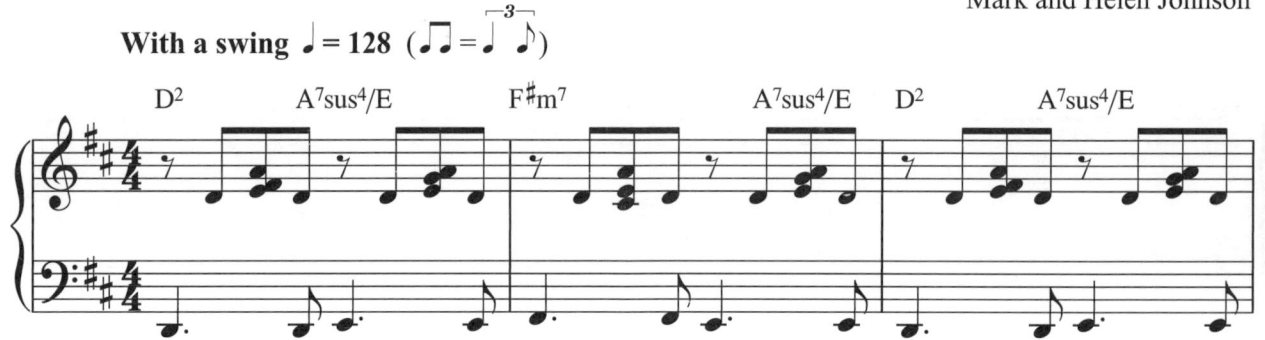

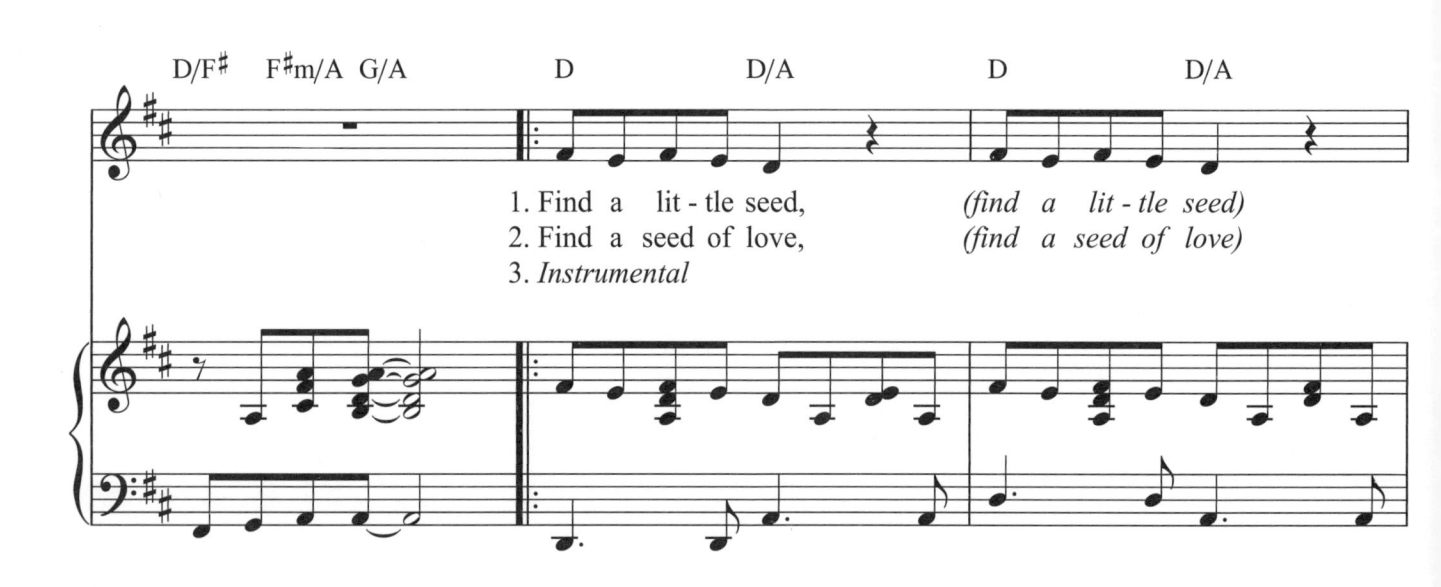

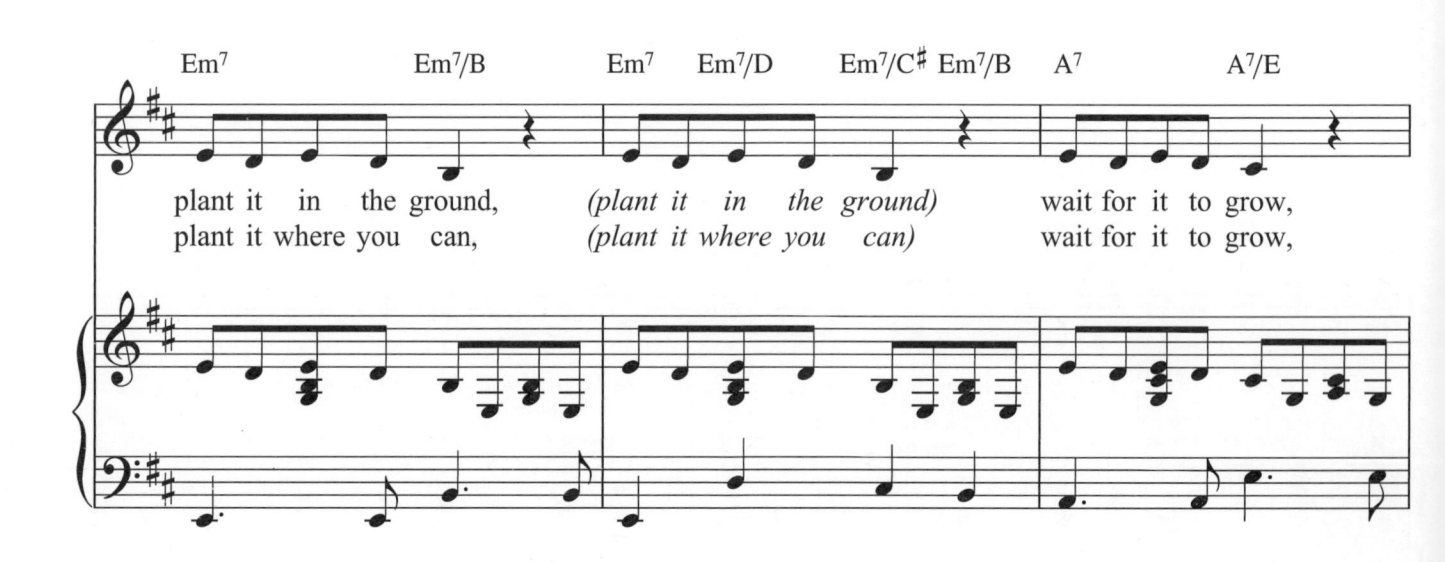

With a swing ♩ = 128

1. Find a lit-tle seed, *(find a lit-tle seed)* plant it in the ground, *(plant it in the ground)* wait for it to grow,
2. Find a seed of love, *(find a seed of love)* plant it where you can, *(plant it where you can)* wait for it to grow,
3. *Instrumental*

© 1995 & 2008 Out of the Ark Ltd, Surrey KT12 4RQ
CCLI Song No. 1574819

(wait for it to grow) don't dis - turb it. Don't ex-pect to see,
(wait for it to grow) don't dis - turb it. Don't ex-pect to see,

(don't ex - pect to see) chan-ges o-ver-night, (chan-ges o-ver-night)
(don't ex - pect to see) chan-ges o-ver-night, (chan-ges over-night)

if you wait a while, (if you wait a while) you'll find new life.
if you wait a while, (if you wait a while) you'll find new life.

Sun-shine will come, rain-drops will fall, your lit-tle seed will

D Cmaj7/E D/F♯ G Em7 F♯m7(♭5) B7
grow a - gain. Soon there will be a day in spring when
Em7 D/A A7
1. 2.
D2 A7sus4/E F♯m7 A7sus4/E
your seed blos-soms and grows.
D2 A7sus4/E D/F♯ F♯m/A G/A
3.
D2 A7sus4/E
grows.
F♯m7 A7sus4/E D2 A7sus4/E N.C. D
And that's that!

SPRING CHICKEN

Words and Music by
Mark and Helen Johnson

With a swing ♩ = 140

Slower, 'straight' quaver feel ♩ = c. 112

1. One mo-ther hen sat on **four** lit-tle eggs,
2. One mo-ther hen sat on **three** lit-tle eggs,
3. One mo-ther hen sat on **two** lit-tle eggs,
4. One mo-ther hen sat on **one** lit-tle egg,

keep-ing them warm in her lit-tle egg nest. Then one day she
keep-ing them warm in her lit-tle egg nest. Then one day she
keep-ing them warm in her lit-tle egg nest. Then one day she
keep-ing it warm in her lit-tle egg nest. Then one day she

© 1995 & 2008 Out of the Ark Ltd, Surrey KT12 4RQ
CCLI Song No. 1574826

27

heard a crack and a lit-tle voice said as the egg was hatched:
fell a-sleep and a lit-tle voice said in a whis-pered tweet:
moved a-bout and a lit-tle voice said as a chick popped out,
gave a sigh and a lit-tle voice said 'SUR-PRISE, SUR-PRISE!!'

Faster, with a swing ♩ = 140

'I'm a spring chic-ken! I'm yel-low and small. My fea-thers are fluf-fy and they're keep-ing me warm. My legs are not long so I'll nev-er be tall, but I'm a

To Coda
1. 2. 3.
F E7/G♯ Am D7/F♯ C/G G7 C
real spring chic - ken and I'm hav - in' a ball!
C5 N.C.
(Chic - ken, I'm a chic - ken, I'm a hav - in' a ball!)'
F E7/G♯ Am D7/F♯ C/G G/B C
4.
C/G G7 C
D.𝄋 al Coda
hav - in' a ball!'
CODA
C/G G/B C C5 N.C. C
hav - in' a ball!
(Chic - ken, I'm a chic - ken, I'm a hav - in' a ball!)'

HOSANNA

Words and Music by
Mark and Helen Johnson

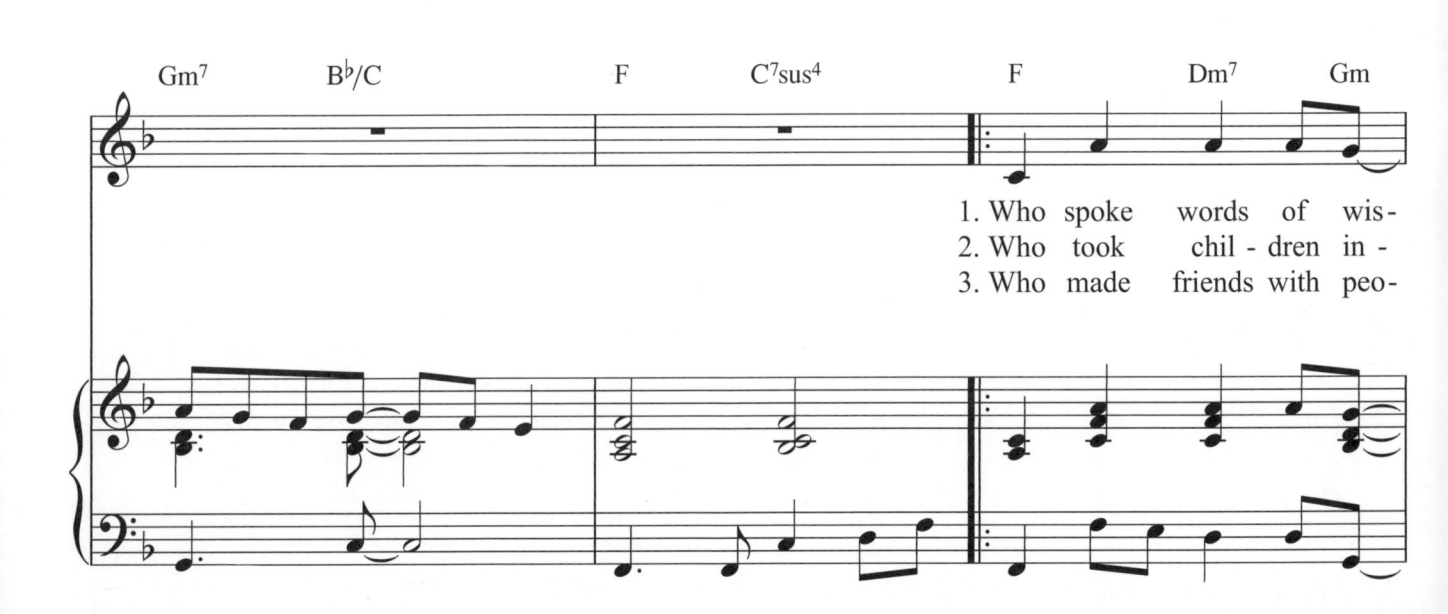

Punchy and positive ♩ = 162

1. Who spoke words of wis-
2. Who took chil-dren in -
3. Who made friends with peo-

© 1995 & 2008 Out of the Ark Ltd, Surrey KT12 4RQ
CCLI Song No. 1574833

- dom and life? *Only the one they call Je - sus.*
- to his arms? *Only the one they call Je - sus.*
- ple des - pised? *Only the one they call Je - sus.*

Under - stood what peo - ple are like? *No - bo - dy o - ther than*
Spoke to storms and made them be calm? *No - bo - dy o - ther than*
Turned the wa - ter in - to good wine? *No - bo - dy o - ther than*

Him. Who per - formed mi - ra - cu - lous signs?
Him. Who raised Laz - 'rus up from the dead?
Him. Who got peo - ple fol - low - ing him?

Only the one they call Jesus. Healed the sick, gave sight to the blind? Nobody other than Him.
Only the one they call Jesus. Made a feast of fishes and bread? Nobody other than Him.
Only the one they call Jesus. Changed their lives, forgave all their sin? Nobody other than Him.

Group 2: Rejoice! Sing praise!

Group 1: Hosanna! Hosanna! Praise Him, come

To Coda
F C/F F B♭/F F C/F
Re - joice!
praise Him! Ho - san - na! Ho - san - na!
1. 2.
3.
D.S. al Coda
Gm7 Gm7/C C7 F C7sus4 F B♭/C
Lift up your voi - ces and sing! Re -
Lift up your voi - ces and sing! sing! Ho -
CODA
rit.
Gm7 C F
Lift up your voi - ces and sing!
Lift up your voi - ces and sing!
Ped.
8vb

EASTER JUBILATION

Words and Music by
Mark and Helen Johnson

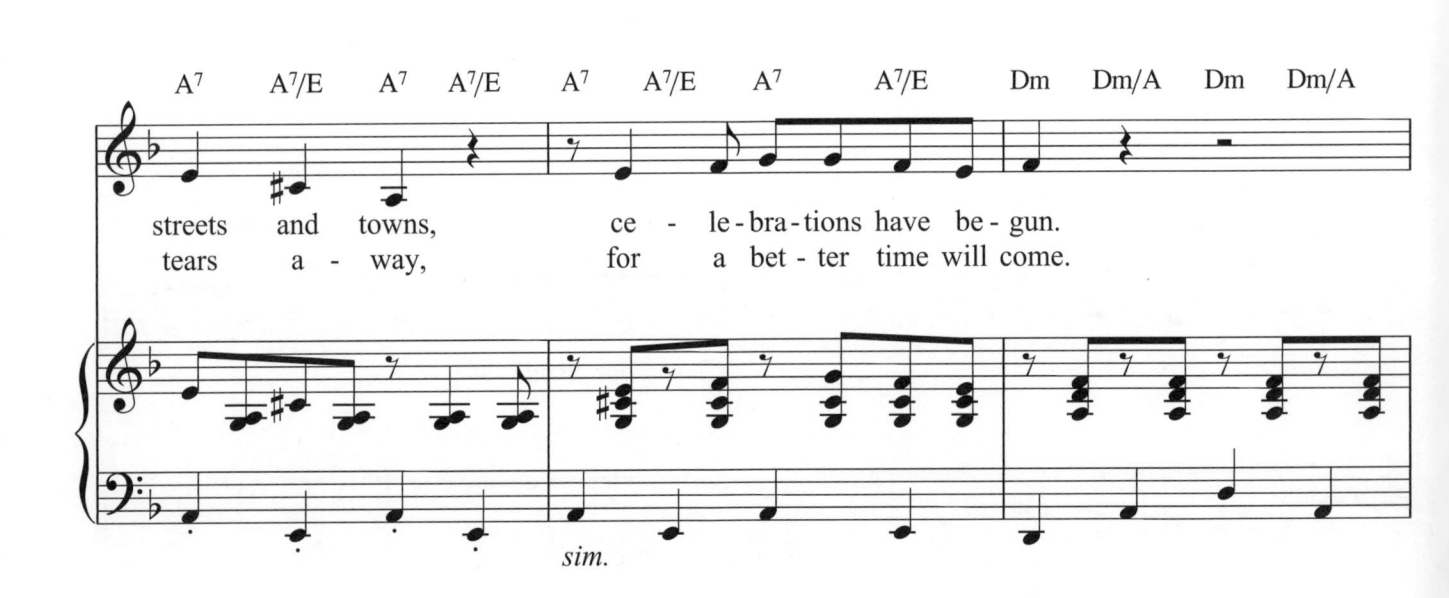

With energy ♩ = 138

1. 4. Easter jubilation fills the streets and towns, celebrations have begun.
2. Put aside your sorrows, wipe your tears away, for a better time will come.
3. La, la, la, la, *etc.*

sim.

© 1995 & 2008 Out of the Ark Ltd, Surrey KT12 4RQ
CCLI Song No. 1574840

Hear the music and the dan - cing now,
There's a pro - mise of a brigh - ter day,

join the laugh-ter and the fun!
join the laugh-ter and the fun!
OH!

Raise a joy - ful shout! Clap your hands and dance, let your

Dm Dm/A D7 D7/A Gm Gm/D Gm Gm/D Dm Dm/A Dm Dm/A
feel - ings out. OH! Hear what it's a-bout,
To Coda
1. 2. 3.
A7 A7/E A7 A7/E Dm A7 Dm Dm/A Dm Dm/A
Christ the Lord has come to set us free!
4.
D.𝄋 al Coda
CODA
Dm Dm/A Dm A7 Dm A7 Dm Dm/A
set us free!
Dm A7 Dm Dm/A
set us free!
A7 A7/E A7 A7/E Dm A7 Dm
Christ the Lord has come to set us free! HEY!

NOW SPRING IS HERE

Words and Music by
Mark and Helen Johnson

Light and bouncy ♩ = 120

1. 4. Spring-time is laugh and sing time, it's join-ing in time, let's give a
2. Lis-ten — the birds are sing-ing, a new be-gin-ning is in the
3. O - ver the pret-ty mea-dows the green and yel-lows are ev-ery-

© 1995 & 2008 Out of the Ark Ltd, Surrey KT12 4RQ
CCLI Song No. 1574857

37

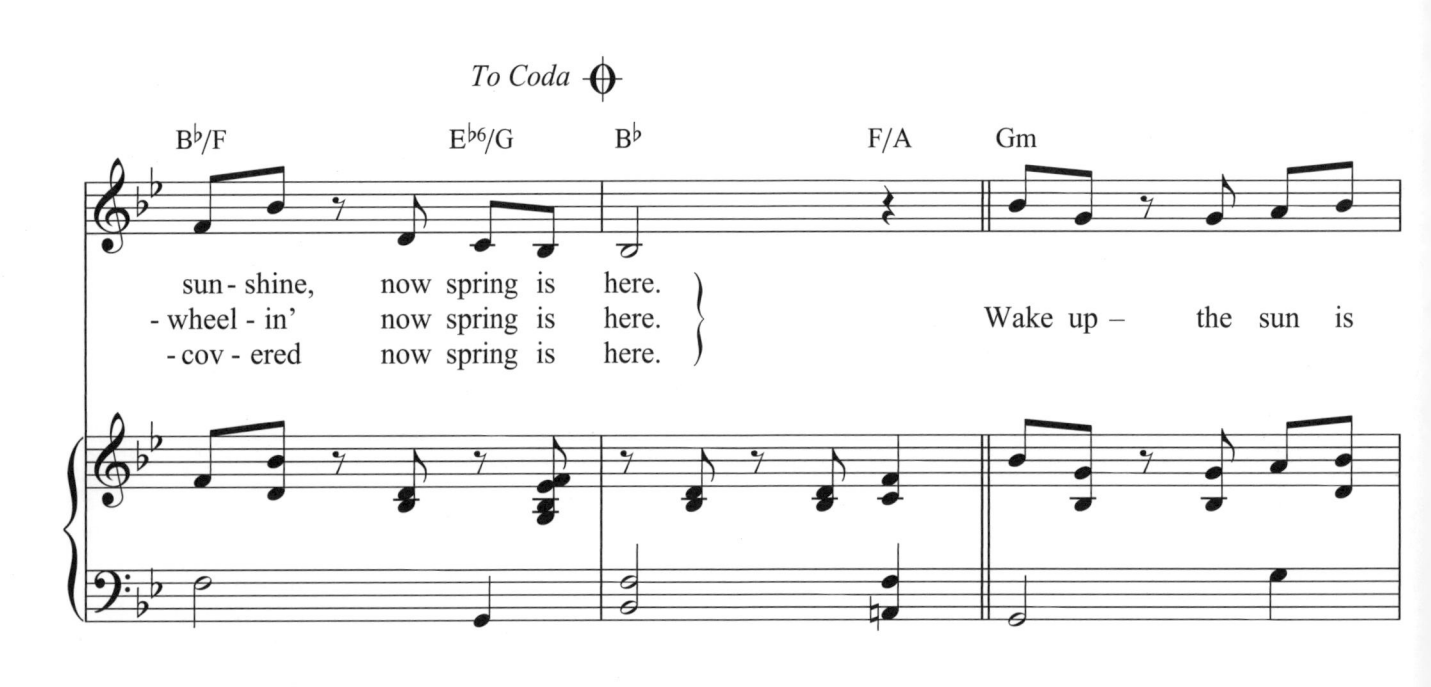

cheer! Join hands and have a fun time, en-joy the
air. Shake off that win-ter feel-ing and go free-
-where. Flo-wers of ev-ery col-our can be dis-

sun-shine, now spring is here.
-wheel-in' now spring is here.
-cov-ered now spring is here.

Wake up — the sun is shi-ning, the earth is smi-ling, the air is clear.

Blue skies are up a-bove me, it's real-ly love-ly this time of

1. 2. year.

3. year. *D.S. al Coda*

CODA

here, now spring is here,

rit.

now spring is here, now spring is here.

THE CHOCOLATE SONG

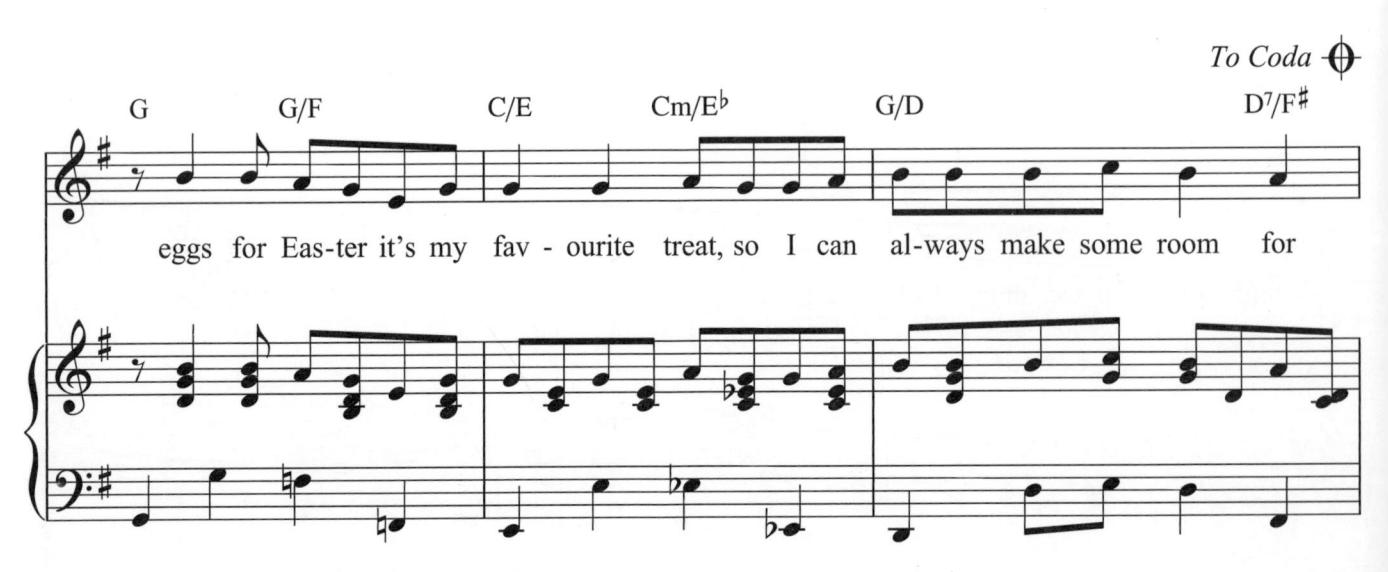

Words and Music by
Mark and Helen Johnson

With a 'country' feel ♩ = 126

Oh I've got lots of choc-olate, give me love-ly choc-olate, it's the best thing to eat, for sure. When I get eggs for Eas-ter it's my fav-ourite treat, so I can al-ways make some room for

To Coda ⊕

© 1995 & 2008 Out of the Ark Ltd, Surrey KT12 4RQ
CCLI Song No. 1574864

1. I've got some plain and milk ones and some toffee-filled ones, I've got boxes all around the place. I've got a strong affection for my chocolate collection, I'm mad about that chocolate taste!

2. I've eaten milky white ones and the sweets inside them, (I've got chocolate all around my face!) They all had pretty wrappers, but that's not what matters, I'm mad about that chocolate taste!

3. I've had some sickly sweet ones and some pretty cheap ones, but I couldn't see them go to waste. I s'pose I should know better, but it's nearly Easter, I'm mad about that chocolate

Oh I've got more!

3. *D.S al Coda* — **CODA**

taste! Oh I've got more! Oh I've got lots of chocolate, give me love-ly choc-olate, it's the best thing to eat for sure. When I get eggs for Eas-ter it's my fav-ourite treat, so I can al-ways make some room for more!

DON'T FORGET
(Mother's Day Song)

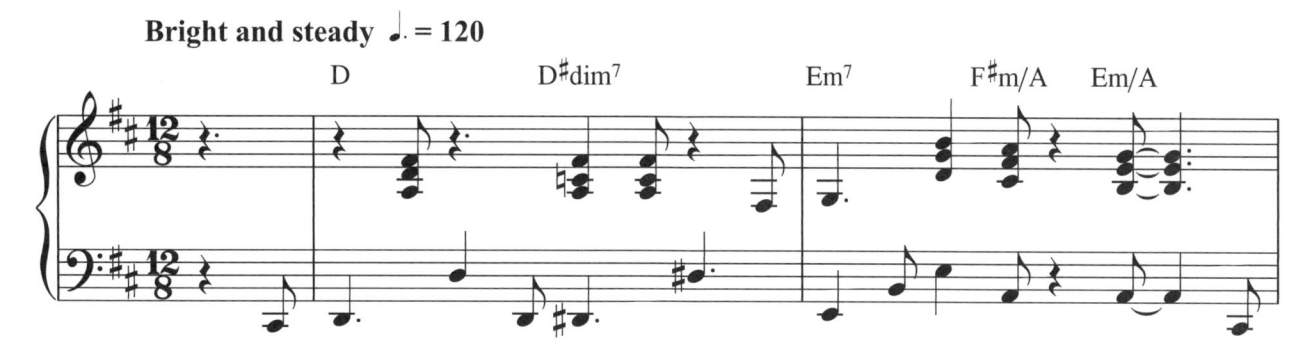

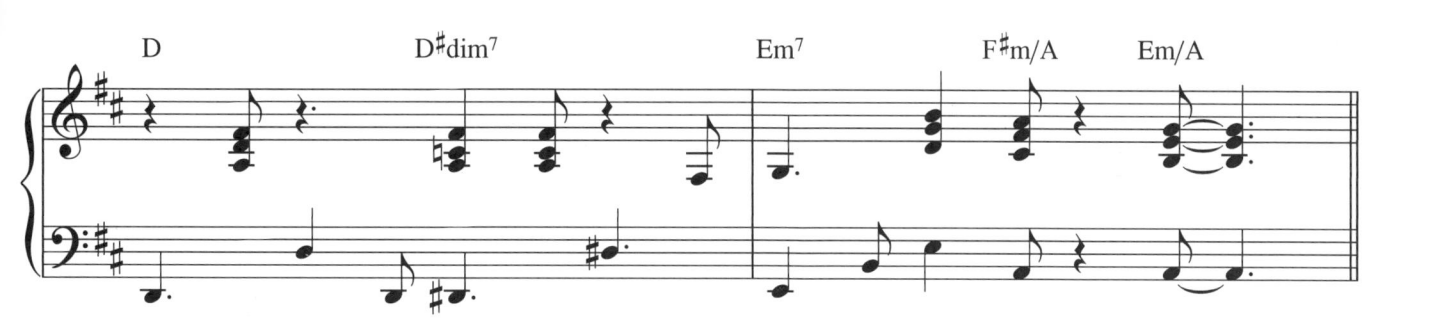

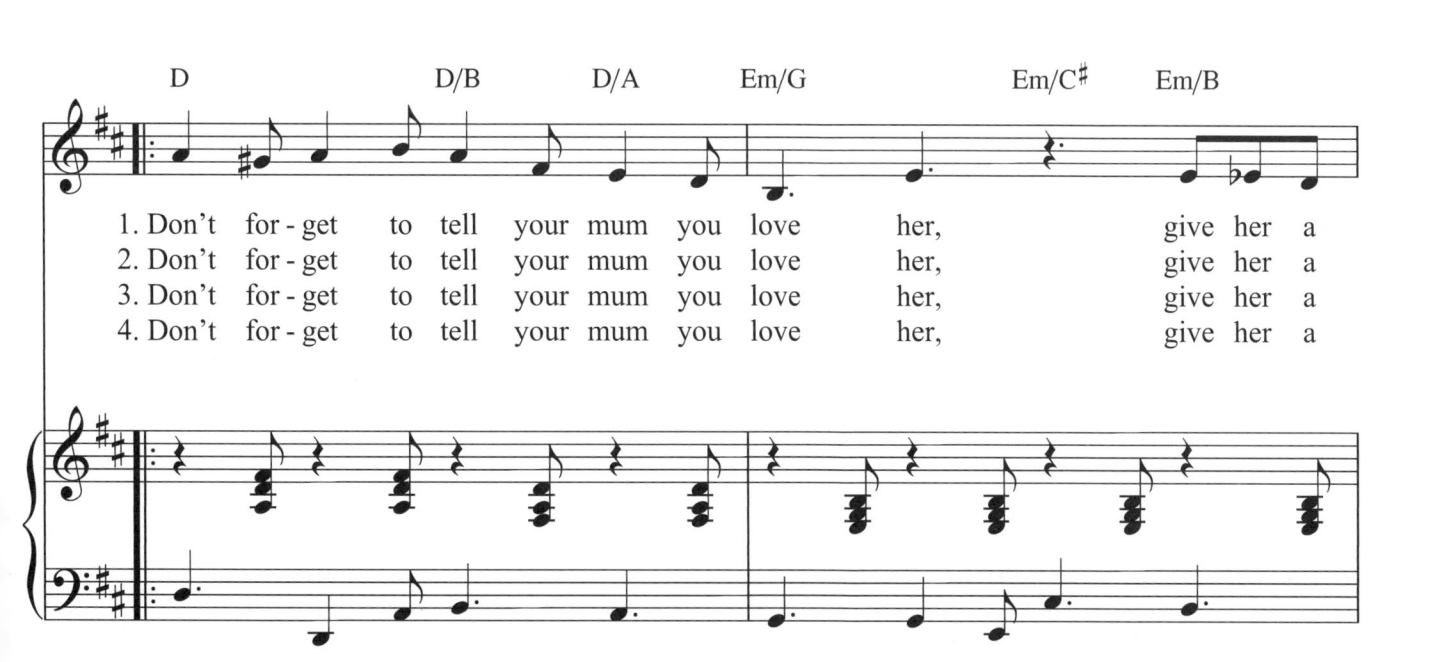

Words and Music by
Mark and Helen Johnson

Bright and steady ♩. = 120

1. Don't for-get to tell your mum you love her, give her a
2. Don't for-get to tell your mum you love her, give her a
3. Don't for-get to tell your mum you love her, give her a
4. Don't for-get to tell your mum you love her, give her a

© 1995 & 2008 Out of the Ark Ltd, Surrey KT12 4RQ
CCLI Song No. 1574871

hug when you get home.
hug when you get home (tell her she's mar - v'lous).
hug when you get home (tell her she's mar - v'lous).
hug when you get home (not ve - ry like - ly).

Don't for - get to tell your mum that she's the best,
Don't for - get to thank her for the things she does,
Don't for - get to give her some - thing real - ly nice,
Don't for - get to help your mum with all the chores,

make her put her feet up – she de - serves a rest!
look - ing af - ter ev - ery - one with - out a fuss!
it's the thought that mat - ters, not the size or price!
clean your bed - room like you've nev - er done be - fore!

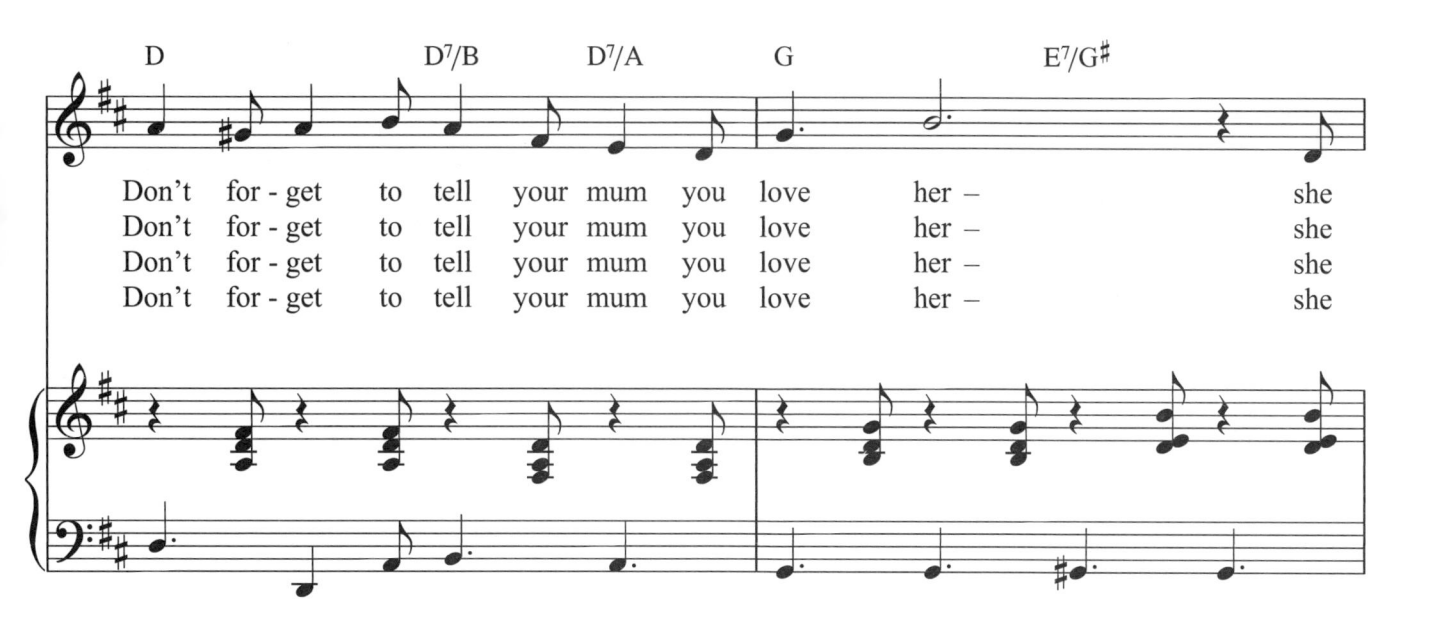

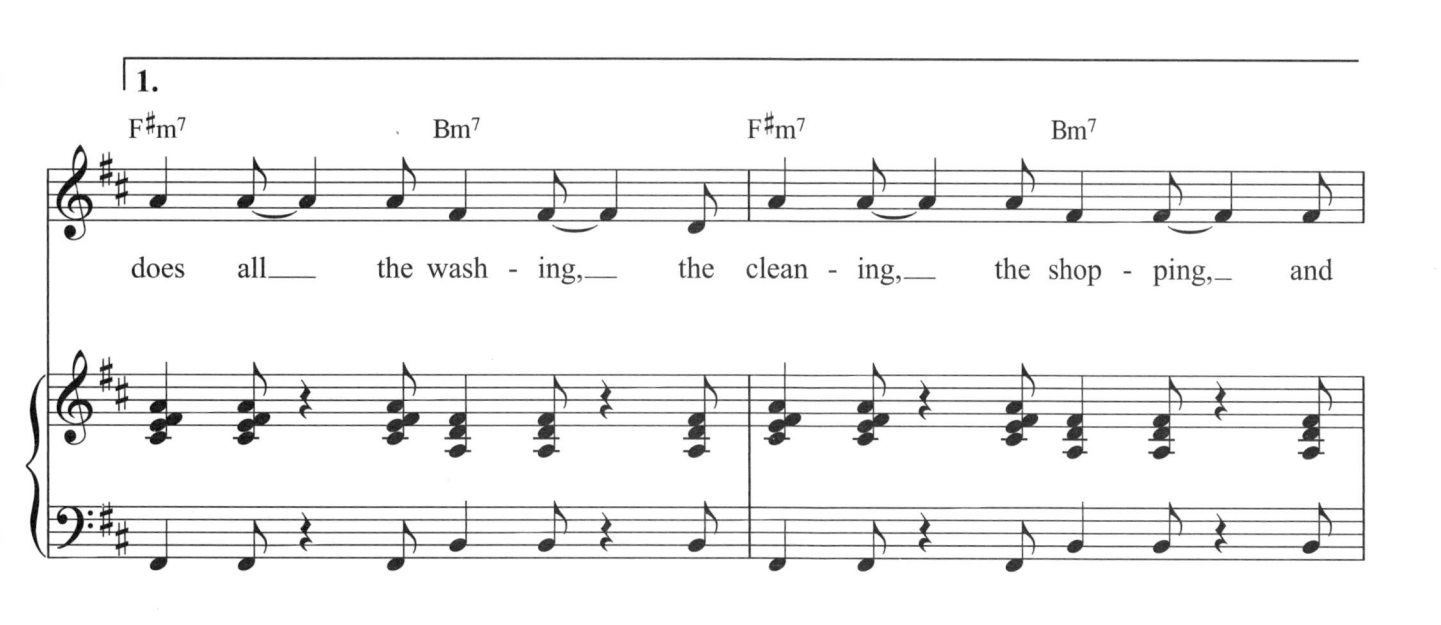

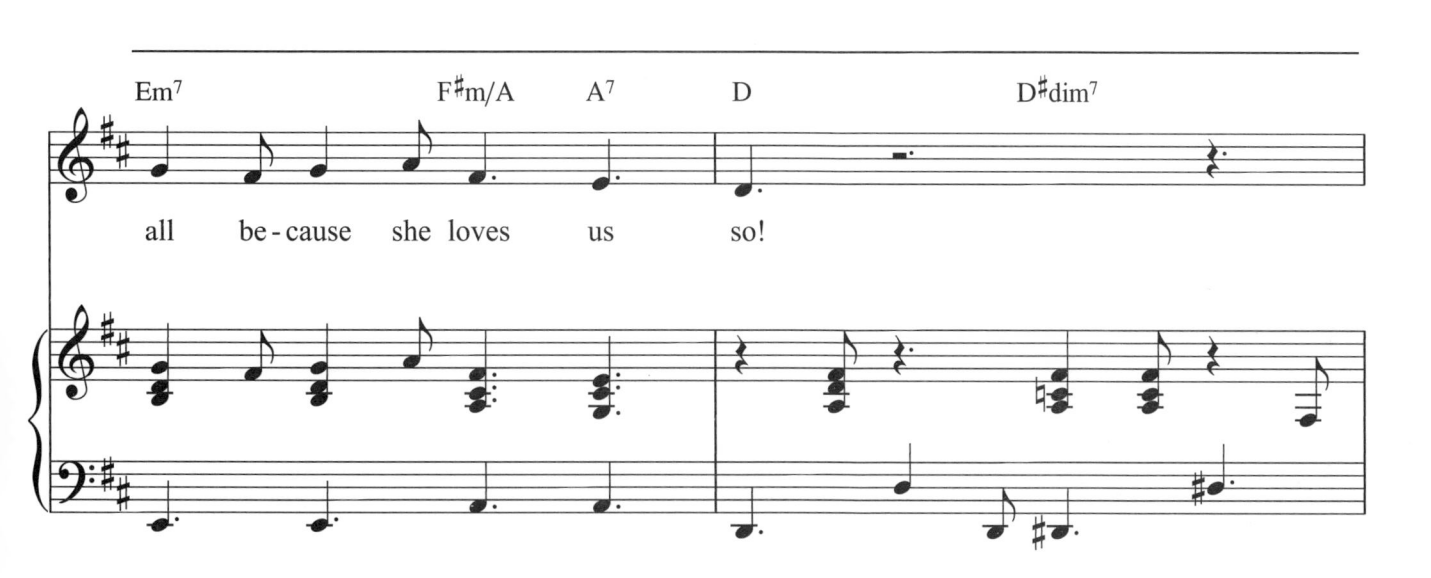

Don't for-get to tell your mum you love her – she
Don't for-get to tell your mum you love her – she
Don't for-get to tell your mum you love her – she
Don't for-get to tell your mum you love her – she

1.

does all the wash-ing, the clean-ing, the shop-ping, and

all be-cause she loves us so!

Em7 F#m/A Em/A D D#dim7 Em7 F#m/A Em/A
2.
F#m7 Bm7 F#m7 Bm7
takes and collects us and makes us our break - fast, she
F#m7 Bm7 F#m7 Bm7
does all the wash - ing, the clean - ing, the shop - ping, and
Em7 F#m/A A7 D D#dim7 Em7 F#m/A Em/A
all be-cause she loves us so!

helps and ad-vi-ses, she gives us sur-pri-ses, she takes and col-lects us and makes us our break-fast, she does all the wash-ing, the clean-ing, the shop-ping, and all be-cause she loves us so!

puts up with rug-by, she knows when to hug me, she helps and ad-vi-ses, she gives us sur-pri-ses, she takes and col-lects us and makes us our break-fast, she

F#m7 Bm7 F#m7 Bm7
does all the wash - ing, the clean - ing, the shop - ping, and
Em7 F#m/A A7 D D#dim7 Em7 F#m/A Em/A
all be-cause she loves us so!
D D#dim7 Em7 F#m/A Em/A D D#dim7
Em7 F#m/A Em/A Em7 F#m/A A7 D A7 D
And all be-cause she loves us so!

MARY'S SONG

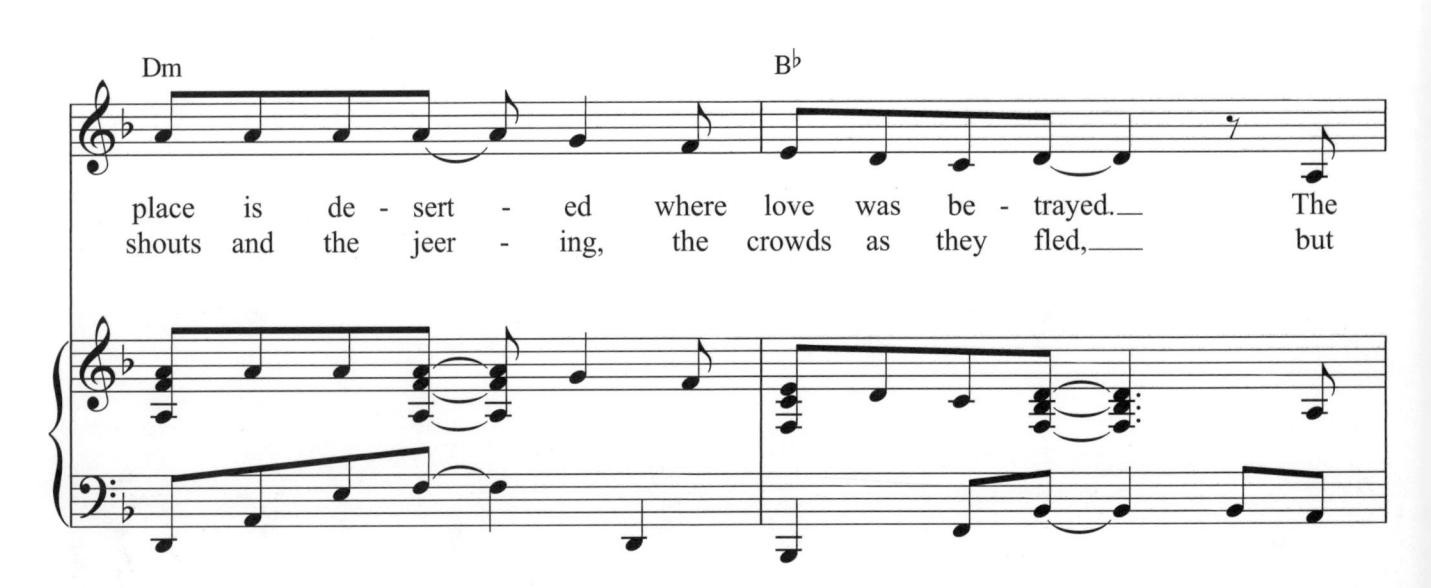

Words and Music by
Mark and Helen Johnson

With feeling ♩ = 84

1. I look to the hillside, the skies have turned grey, this place is deserted where love was betrayed. The
(3.) noises still echo around in my head, the shouts and the jeering, the crowds as they fled, but

© 1995 & 2008 Out of the Ark Ltd, Surrey KT12 4RQ
CCLI Song No. 1574888

life you gave free-ly was ta-ken from me___ to-day.___
now it's all o-ver and I'm on my own___ a-gain.___

2. I see it so clear-ly, the
4. I grate-ful-ly bore_ you, I

look on your face,___ the sad-ness and sor-row, the
watched as you grew,___ I lis-tened and won-dered at

pain you em - braced,___ and now it's all o - ver, a
all that you knew,___ but this is the hard - est of

si - lence en - folds___ the day.___
all that I've learned___ from you.___

Tell me

why did it have___ to be done, when my feel-ings of love___ are so

To Coda
C2 C Gm7 F E♭(♮4+2) Dm7
strong? Could it be there's a rea - son for tak-ing the life of my
1. 2.
Csus4 C Csus4
son? 3. The son?
D.𝄋 al Coda
CODA
C Gm/B♭ F/A
Tell me
Gsus4 rit. G2 G
son?

WHEN I THINK ABOUT THE CROSS

(Dedicated to Stanley and Doreen Voke)

Words and Music by
Mark and Helen Johnson

Contemplative ♩ = 128

1º + 2º: Solo
3º: All

When I think a-bout the cross, when I think of Je-sus, I'm re-mind-ed of His love – love that

© 1995 & 2008 Out of the Ark Ltd, Surrey KT12 4RQ
CCLI Song No. 1574895

never leaves me. Who am I that He should die, giving life so freely? When I think about the cross, help me to believe it. it.

CELEBRATE

Words and Music by
Mark and Helen Johnson

Bright and bouncy ♩ = 155

1. 6. Sing a song, sing a joyful song, sing a joyful song to
2. Clap your hands, clap your hands like this, clap your hands like this to
3. Jump up and down, up and down and a-round, up and down and a-round to
4. Dance to the beat, to the beat of the drum, to the beat of the drum to
5. Wave your hands, wave your hands in the air, wave your hands in the air to

To Coda

ce-le-brate! Sing a song, sing a joyful song, sing a
ce-le-brate! Clap your hands, clap your hands like this, clap your
ce-le-brate! Jump up and down, up and down and a-round, up and
ce-le-brate! Dance to the beat, to the beat of the drum, to the
ce-le-brate! Wave your hands, wave your hands in the air, wave your

© 1995 & 2008 Out of the Ark Ltd, Surrey KT12 4RQ
CCLI Song No. 1574905

joy - ful song to ce - le - brate!
hands like this to ce - le - brate!
down and a - round to ce - le - brate!
beat of the drum to ce - le - brate!
hands in the air to ce - le - brate!

Je - sus is a - live,— you know, He's ris - en from the dead.—

He was cru - ci - fied— but now He's ris - en like He said!

1 – 4. (Hal - le - lu - jah!)

5. *D.S. al Coda* (Hal - le - lu - jah!)

CODA

joy - ful song to ce - le - brate!

RISEN!

*Words and Music by
Mark and Helen Johnson*

Punchy and positive ♩ = 168

Ris - en! Ris - en! Je - sus is ris - en! The Spi - rit was giv - en —

© 1995 & 2008 Out of the Ark Ltd, Surrey KT12 4RQ
CCLI Song No. 1574912

Jesus is a-live! Ris - en! Ris - en!

Jesus is risen! The Spi - rit was giv - en —

Jesus is a-live!

1. Ear - ly in the morn - ing on the
2. Fear - ful and ex - ci - ted, a -
3. Two of the be - liev - ers, with
4. All of his dis - ci - ples were

first day of the week, wo-men went to vi-
-mazed by all they'd seen, Ma-ry and her friends
thoughts a-bout the week, walked the road so lone-
ter-ri-fied to see Je-sus there be-fore

-sit at the tomb.
ran from the tomb.
-ly and con-fused.
them in the room.

An-gels came and told them, 'The one you've come to see,
Find-ing the dis-ci-ples to-ge-ther where they'd meet,
While they spoke of Je-sus and all he'd come to mean,
'Why are you so fright-ened?' He said, 'It's real-ly me!

He is-n't here but you will meet Him soon!'
burst-ing with joy they ran in-to the room!
He came a-long be-side them with the news:
All of the things I told you have come true!'

CODA

Je-sus is a-live!

Ris-en! Ris-en! Je-sus is ris-en!

THE GIFT OF LIFE

> We have provided an outline notation for the verse and chorus, however effective performance of this rap will require use of the backing track.

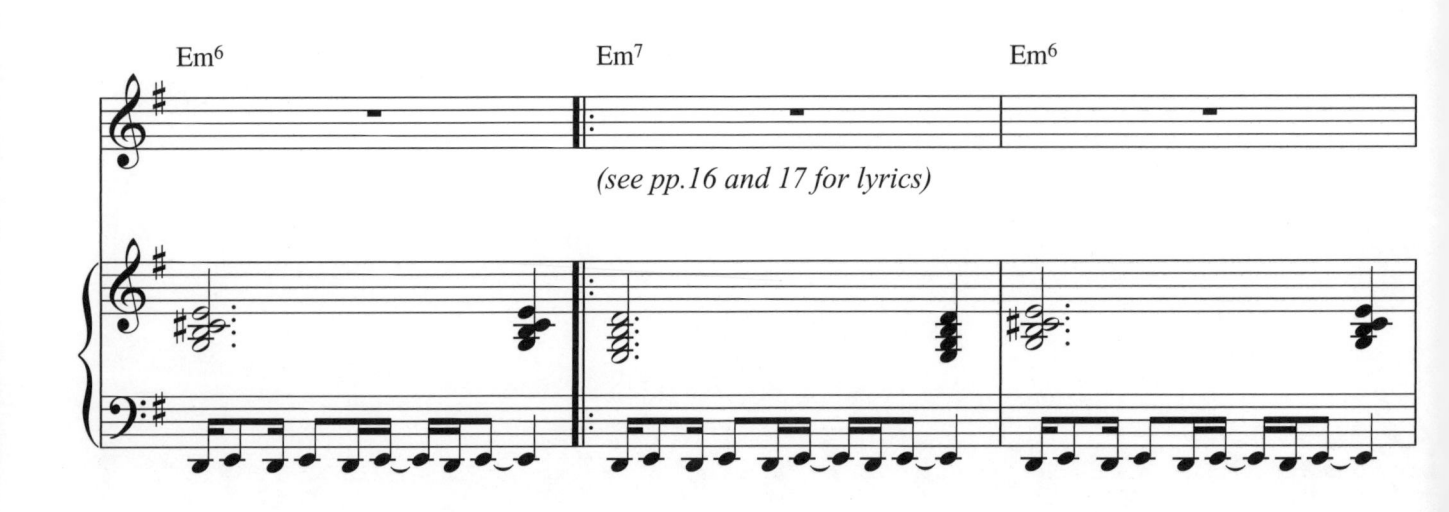

Words and Music by
Mark and Helen Johnson

With attitude ♩ = 92

(see pp.16 and 17 for lyrics)

© 1995 & 2008 Out of the Ark Ltd, Surrey KT12 4RQ
CCLI Song No. 1574929

63

THANK YOU FOR LOVING ME

*Words and Music by
Mark and Helen Johnson*

Smoothly ♩ = 128

1. Before you made the skies and sea your heart was full of love for me, you knew the person I would be, thank you for loving

me. 2. You came to earth to live like us, with
(3.) - cause God loved the world so much you
(4. *Instrumental*)

words of life and arms of love, you showed the way to
paid the price for all of us, you gave your life up-

heav'n a - bove, thank you for lov - ing us.
- on a cross, thank you for lov - ing us.

Thank you Je - sus, thank you my Lord. Your love came down from hea - ven, come fill up my heart ev - er - more.

2.
D.𝄋 al Coda
A2/E E A2/E A2/E E A2/E
3. Be -
4. Instrumental
CODA
A2/E E F♯m7 A6 B
5. So thank you Lord for lov - ing me, to -
F♯m7 B2 B A2/C♯ B/D♯ E F♯m7
- day and all e - ter - ni - ty, and may my song for -
A6 G♯7 F♯m7 B7sus4 E
- ev - er be 'Thank you for lov - ing me'.

Thank you Je-sus, thank you my Lord. Your love came down from hea-ven, come fill up my heart ev-er-more. more.

HE'S ALIVE!

Words and Music by
Mark and Helen Johnson

Triumphantly ♩. = 62

Come and join in the song, Jesus Christ is Lord over all, and He lives to reign forever more, the heavens applaud, 'He's alive!'

© 1995 & 2008 Out of the Ark Ltd, Surrey KT12 4RQ
CCLI Song No. 1574943

He's a-live!'

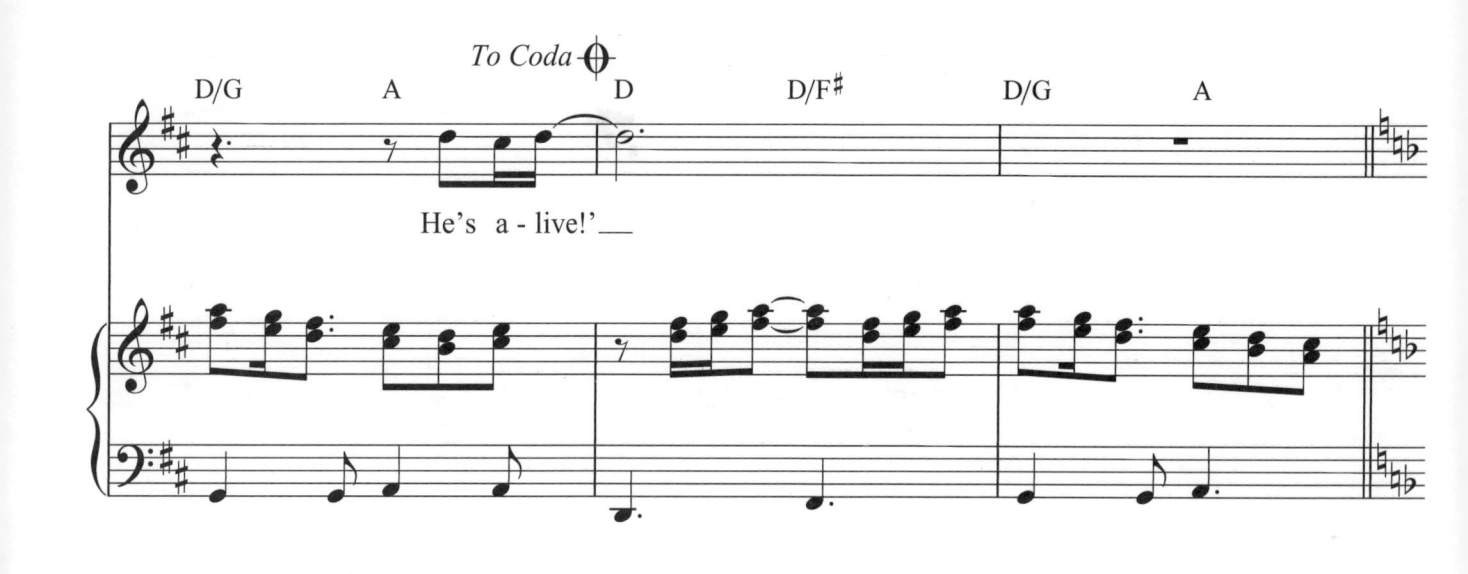

1. Lift your hearts and your voi-ces, fill the
2. Lift your hearts and your voi-ces, fill the
3. Lift your hearts and your voi-ces, fill the

earth with re-joic-ing for He's as-cen-ded to the skies, in
earth with re-joic-ing for ev-ery knee shall bow to Him and
earth with re-joic-ing for ev-ery na-tion, ev-ery tribe will

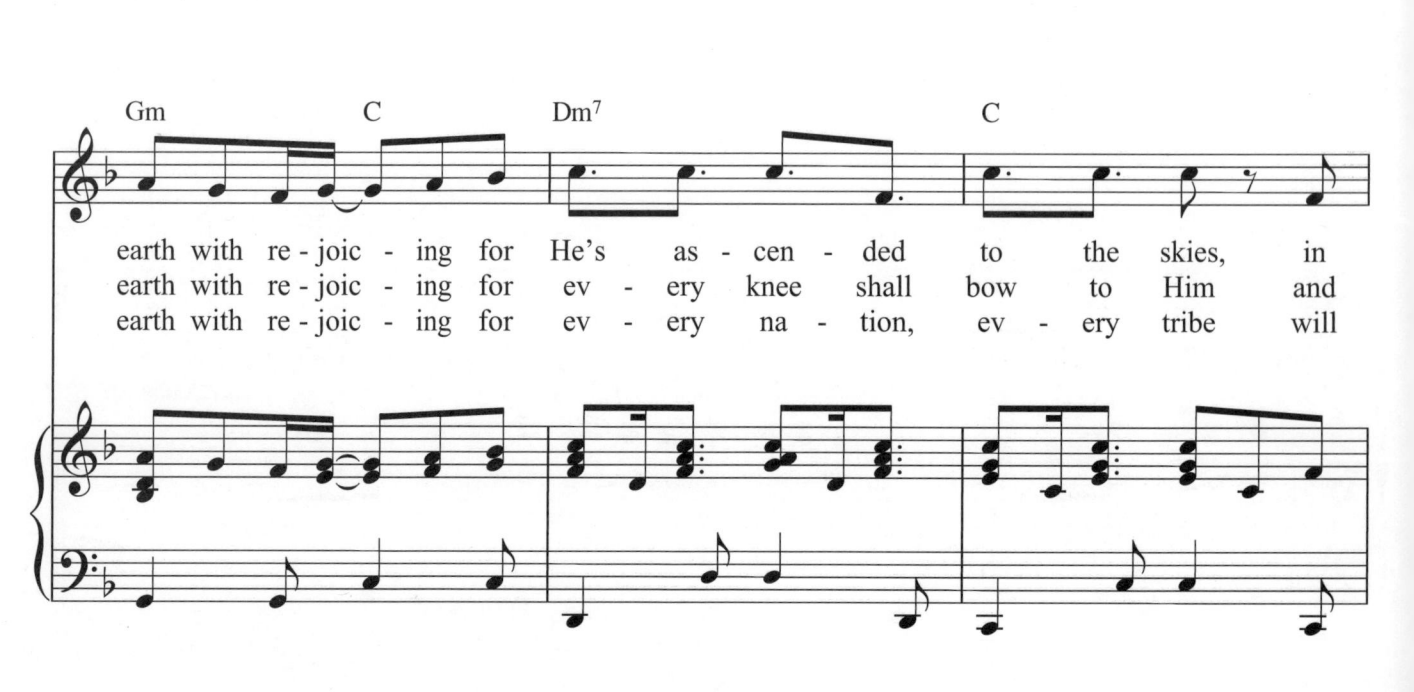

heaven now He reigns. Lord of glory,
ev - ery - one con - fess: Je - sus Christ is
glo - ri - fy His name. All cre - a - tion

Lord of life, He will re - turn a - gain!
Lord and King, He's con - quered sin and death!
shall bow down and hon - our Him with praise!

D.S. al Coda

CODA

'He's a - live!___ He's a - live!'

COPYRIGHT & LICENSING

The world of copyright and licensing can seem rather daunting. Whilst it is a legal requirement for schools to comply with copyright law, we recognise that teachers are extremely busy. For this reason we try to make the process of compliance as simple as possible. The guidelines below explain the most common copyright and licensing issues.

Helpful information can be found on the following website:
A Guide to Licensing Copyright in Schools
www.licensing-copyright.org

And remember, we are always happy to help. For advice simply contact our customer services team:
UK: 01932 232 250   International: +44 1932 232 250   copyright@outoftheark.com

GENERAL GUIDELINES

You are free to use the material in our songbooks for all **teaching purposes**. However the **reproduction** of lyrics and/or music scores (whether for classroom, assembly or collective worship use) and the **performance** of songs to an audience are both subject to licensing requirements by law. The key points are set out below:

Reproduction of Song Lyrics or Musical Scores

The following licences from Christian Copyright Licensing Ltd (www.ccli.com) permit photocopying or reproduction of song lyrics and music scores, for example to create song-sheets, overhead transparencies or to display the lyrics or music using any electronic medium.

For UK schools: A Collective Worship Copyright Licence and a Music Reproduction Licence.
For churches: A Church Copyright and Music Reproduction Licence.

The following credit should be included with the lyrics:
'Reproduced by kind permission © Out of the Ark Ltd'

Please ensure that you log the songs that are used on your copy report. (Organisations that do not hold one of the above licences should contact Out of the Ark Music directly for permission.)

> **A licence IS required by law if you:**
> - Make photocopies of lyrics
> - Create overhead transparencies of lyrics
> - Type lyrics into a computer file
> - Display lyrics on an interactive whiteboard

PERFORMANCE OF SONGS

If you are performing any of our songs for the public on school premises (i.e. for anybody other than staff and pupils) then royalty payments become due.

Most schools have an arrangement with the Performing Rights Society (PRS) through their local authority. Organisations that do not have such an arrangement should contact Out of the Ark Music directly. The PRS licence does not cover musicals.

Note: If you are staging one of our musicals or nativity plays then a performance licence issued by Out of the Ark Music is required. This licence covers the performance of the songs from the musical.

AUDIO AND VIDEO RECORDINGS

If you wish to make an audio or video recording of any of our works please contact us directly:
UK: 01932 232 250   International: +44 1932 232 250   copyright@outoftheark.com